RECOVERING MY SANITY

POEMS and SHORT STORIES

Δ

BEECHER SMITH

Zapizdat Publications

Palo Alto, 1996

Copyright © 1995, D. Beecher Smith, II
Printed in the United States of America

All material contained herein is the original work of the author and may not be reproduced in whole or in part without his express written permission

A ZAPIZDAT PUBLICATION

in conjunction with

HOT BISCUIT PRODUCTIONS, INC.

ISBN 1-880964-16-3

ZAPIZDAT PUBLICATIONS
P. O. Box 326
Palo Alto, CA 94302

CONTENTS

Part I: Poems 9

Recovering My Sanity	11
Bedazzled	12
Response	13
Forever Friends	14
Last October	15
The Psychiatrist's Patients' Pet Peeves . .	16
Grandpa Frank and His Bostons . . .	17
Resolution	20
Custer's Mistress	21
Vanpyr	22
To Lady	23
Blanche Cole	25
Lucifer's Carol	26
The King Of Smiles	27
The Wilderness Temptation	28
Dark Angel	29
Lilith on the Mall	32
Cold Gray Thanksgiving Day . . .	34
Debbie's White Christmas	35
Morning at East Elementary School . .	36
Traitor	37
Facing the Fear	39
Uh-Oh!	41
Show Me the Way	42
The Void	44
Paulie the Parrot	45
Garfield's Gut	46
Into the Light	47
After the "Wilding"	49
Summer Storm	50
The Day I Met the Famous Writer… . .	51
Ghia's Lesson	52
Melvin's Message	54
Reunion Reflection	55
Esau Remembers	56
To Winifred For "Pepe" and "Nitro" . .	57
Cassie's Curse	59
Haiku	60
Waiting on a Wet Balcony	61

Consolation Prize 62
Adieu 63

Credits 65

Part II: Stories 69

The Burrower From the Bluff 71
Due Process 81
Return of the King 89

Credits 95

POEMS

RECOVERING MY SANITY

recovering my sanity requires
more than a few forced memory lapses
when I see you return from the grocery
to your apartment across the hall
      smile at me briefly, weakly, insincerely
           acknowledge my existence from a distance
the cool safe barrier of twenty feet
fearful to engage in talk that might suggest
      possibilities still exist—
           longing for what could make me forget
the fragrance of your Obsession

recovering my sanity requires
prioritizing the future to prevent
unrealistic expectations
of resurrecting our relationship—
accepting that I shall miss
stolen moments when we nakedly ignored
      the grit beneath your kitchen table
           splinters in the hallway floor
                 mothballs on the closet shelf
your cat watching us—
me remembering you have someone already
and I was just an interlude

recovering my sanity requires
understanding two apart can love less painfully
that obligations
      are sometimes stronger
           than emotions
and security means more past forty—something
recovering my sanity requires

BEDAZZLED

On a rainy, wet September afternoon,
My heart leaped when
She
No more than nineteen
Glided into the college reception
And blew me away
With her smile.

No force on earth
Is more powerful than
Innocence:

No innocence
More beautiful than
That kept by choice.

At forty-four, a professor,
I am too old in appearance
To do anything socially acceptable
Except admire her, yet
I still thank God for
Such infinite variety
In beauty
And the opportunity
To share it safely.

But I also know
How Faustus felt,
So willing to bargain his soul,
When Mephistopheles showed him Marguerite
(And I also give thanks that
There really is no such Tempter,
For I, too, would have gladly yielded
To such Magic!)

RESPONSE

Although I call, you will not come;
You weren't like that yesterday;
I know you still respond for some.

Your love seemed like the sweetest plum
Plucked with kisses from our play.
Although I call, you will not come.

You claim that I was just a chum;
Commitment costs too much, you say;
I know you still respond for some.

Desire beats in me like a drum;
But you took the music away—
Although I call, you will not come.

There is no solace found in rum—
It can't make blue skies out of gray;
I know you still respond for some.

This hope still helps me to be strong—
That you'll come back some sunny day;
Although I call, you will not come;
I know you still respond for some.

FOREVER FRIENDS

You once said that, if I hurt you,
We could always make amends;
I vowed then not to desert you—
We would be forever friends.

Talk came so easily with you
On subjects without ends—
How could I not believe it true
We would be forever friends?

When lust and greed got through to you,
I came for your defense—
Though I tried and vied and failed, I knew
We would be forever friends.

You tell me not to bother you;
That nothing now depends
On trust between us—we are through—
There are no forever friends.

(But if, by chance, you called anew,
I'd turn the world up-ends,
And do anything to prove to you
We should be forever friends.)

LAST OCTOBER

Last October it didn't rain at harvest,
So your father won his wager
Against nature, the boll weevils, and the bank.

Chapel Hill had accepted me
For full scholarship at graduate school
And I thought the nation needed
More poets than Animal Husbandry majors.

When I came visiting last October,
You weren't sure where
Our relationship was headed,
But said you needed to know.

We rode around and watched in wonder
As the combine collected the beans,
Counted as the corn stalks fell row by row,
Thanked God for the dry weather
As the automated cotton picker plucked.

We stared at your father, stooped at 48,
Temporarily triumphant,
Still smoking Camels against his doctor's advice,
Celebrating his bumper crop with a Budweiser.

You told me about the lump
The doctor found on his lung.
I told you I could not be here next year.

At the door you kissed me goodby;
I hugged you and looked into your eyes—
Those once-hungry eyes that used to say,
"You're all I want, all I'll ever need;"
But now say, "I don't know."

"I still love you," you confessed.
But what good is that, when it's over?

THE PSYCHIATRIST'S PATIENTS' PET PEEVES

(With profoundest apologies to Dorothy Parker, Ogden Nash, and Shel Silverstein)

Sandy hates all snakes,
Seymore spurns most salad oils,
Wilda wails at wakes,
And Blackie hates his boils.

Tommy hates loud talkers,
Joseph hates a jerk,
Fanny shuns fast walkers
And William hates to work.

Larry hates late charges,
Connie hates the cold,
Dickens hates DeFarges;
While Gramps hates growing old.

Chester hates all cheapskates,
Phillip hates all phonies;
Sam hates losing sweepstakes
And not placing with the ponies.

Henny hates his honey
'Cause she left him at the ball;
Doc Moore *loves* the money
From listening to them all.

GRANDPA FRANK AND HIS BOSTONS

Nobody really loved Grandpa Frank,
Not like they were supposed to—
Except Peppy, Brutus, Ginger, and Judy,
His four Boston Terriers,
Who were more mean than he was
And, as a mad-dog trial lawyer,
He respected anything meaner,
Or, nastier,
Like little Judy with her spastic stomach,
Who was always spitting up—
Usually on Grandma's best rug.

When he set us to work whitewashing
His picket fence,
Sister Winnie, in true Tom Sawyer fashion,
Basted Judy's behind;
Grandpa Frank heard her yelp;
He noticed her rear end was much whiter,
And went for his twelve-gauge, telling us,
"I don't care which of you did it,
I'm gonna blast all of you!"

We didn't think he really meant it,
But he still scared us.

Same way with the back yard rabbits:
They frightened Judy,
So Grandpa Frank opened up on them
With both barrels for terrorizing his darling.

When mice invaded their home,
He told Grandma to put out rat bait—
Carefully, so the Bostons wouldn't find it—
Two of them did anyway;
The shock frightened Grandma so bad
She forgot which ones;
All had to have their stomachs pumped—
Equality among the "little uglies."

17

Our dad, Frank Jr., wanted to be a lawyer, too;
He went to night law school,
Selling automotive appliances by day.
In a rare fit of kindness,
Grandpa Frank bought four new tires
And a T.V. set to help Dad—
On credit, so he'd get a higher commission.

A month passed and Grandpa Frank
Forgot about the first installment.
The store's credit manager asked Frank Jr.,
"What about your father's delinquent account?"
Dad wrote in red ink across the ledger
"REPOSSESS."

Saturday night, the Sheriff came knocking
While our grandparents were readying for a formal dinner.
He'd placed Grandpa's Continental on blocks,
Taken the tires, and then demanded the T.V. set.
It was months before Grandpa
Stopped making death threats
Against Frank Jr.

Ham, a law partner, would come by the house
Stinking drunk every Christmas Eve;
If Grandpa wasn't home,
Ham would rile the four little feists
While he waited.
One year Ham teased the Bostons too much—
They bit his hand, and it bled badly;
Grandma caught Grandpa Frank arriving
Later (and drunker) than Ham;
She warned about his partner's injury.
"Call the vet," Grandpa shouted,
"We might still be able
To save some of the dogs!"

Frank's doctor told him to quit
Drinking, smoking, and get rid of the dogs,
As all affected his asthma;
He told the doc to go to hell,
And obtained a second opinion.

Six months later,
When Grandpa Frank passed away,
His four small charges, who never cared
About anything except three square meals and
Constant 68-degree room temperature,
Quit eating, and had to be
Put to sleep.

RESOLUTION

Lunatics laugh in their loneliness.
Lost and alone, I could cry.
Losing all hope in our dream of togetherness
Only makes me wonder, why?

This much I know: It was.
Though it might not be again.
And trusting in just such a cause
Is the folly of arrogant men.

So, I'll not hope that the sun shines,
Nor wish for no clouds up above.
Alone, in the shade of these pines,
I will pray for your lingering love.

But, if you should leave me tomorrow,
I won't dry for the breeze like the chaff.
Instead, I'll go drown all my sorrow
In sunshine. And, maybe, you'll hear me laugh!

CUSTER'S MISTRESS

The Son of the Morning Star
Visited my village on the Washita
Before dawn on his Thanksgiving Day
Not knowing our chief was Black Kettle,
A friend to the white men.

To them we were all just Indians
And only good if dead.

Yellow Hair, breaker of treaties,
Sent most of my family
To the Spirit World that snowy morning,
But spared me.

Although already with child,
He took me for his mistress.
"Me-o-tsi" was too hard for him to say
So I became "Monacita."
My body was his, but not my spirit.

For five years he kept me
Hidden from Libbie, but no secret
To the regiment. In time I bore him
His only son, Yellow Hawk.

He tired of me and I returned to my people,
Raised our child in the Red Man's ways,
And chanced to be near the Little Big Horn
When my ex-lover made his last stand.

For our son's sake
No tomahawk claimed Custer's scalp.
His goods were taken, but his body left alone,
Except that our women pierced his eardrums
So he would listen better
In the next life.

VAMPYR

Night falls,
Earth moves;
He rises.

Wind blows,
Moon shines;
He soars.

Wing borne,
He lights;
She dreams.

Blood flows—
Passion;
He feeds.

Death comes—
Rapture!
He flies.

Day breaks,
Earth moves;
He sleeps.

TO LADY

More head than body, still tiny
At eight weeks, I found you:
As black-and-white as a Firestone radial
And tougher than steel belt,
For after all, you were a Boston Terrier;
Love at first sight (and first bite,
'Cause you were teething).

Your cute ugliness melted my
Girlfriend's heart before I could;
That endeared you all the more to both of us;
And with me just out of college that summer,
Not wanting to work anyway, needing to teach you
Housebreaking and fetching lessons —
You were the perfect excuse!

At law school, while others went mad,
Your company kept me sane;
Cold winter mornings found you
Scrunched against my warm outer bedcovers,
Making winning legal arguments
With your soulful brown eyes
Against rising too quickly.

Then came marriage, children
And a busy law practice —
No time anymore for my big puppy
Grown old, arthritic, sedentary;
One morning a coward from The Dog Pound
Kidnapped you
While you slept in our side yard —
I had to bail you out like a common criminal —
You became my client.

Death beckoned, but you would not leave me;
He cheated: taking your mind first,
Leaving you lame and incontinent —
The vet provided the ultimate cure.

In the shady backyard we buried you—
Marble tombstone and wooden casket—
Flaunting city ordinances for our lost loved one
And I bawled like a baby
For three days.

BLANCHE COLE
(a *Spoon River Anthology* style poem)

Daddy, a simple farmer, told me
To stop dreaming about Paris and Rome;
Forget my high-falutin' fancies
And get used to seeing the red Georgia clay,
The farthest I would get might be Atlanta.

Then I met you Billy Bucklough —
Handsome, smooth-talking traveling salesman,
Who showed up at the church picnic
For free fried chicken
And some female company —
You said you shared my dreams of seeing the world.

After listening to your stories of Memphis,
New Orleans, and New York,
I knew Columbus couldn't hold me;
I was ready for love and leaving,
Ready to jump into your strong arms
And drown in your blue eyes.

It seemed like a bad dream
When I awoke alone in that Atlanta hotel room
And realized you'd left;
Your good-by note was no consolation,
Neither was the fifty-dollar bill on the dresser.

Before the train could take me
Back to shame and disgrace in Columbus
I decided to exchange my ticket
For a more permanent destination.

As the iron wheels of the engine
Embraced me, I cursed you, Billy, for leaving,
And myself for not listening, and
My daddy for being right
About Atlanta.

LUCIFER'S CAROL

I cannot sing "O Holy Night,"
I cannot love
The unfallen stars so brightly shining;
"Our Dear Savior's birth"
Does nothing to assuage
My loneliness.

I laugh aloud at black Johnny Mathis
Singing about White Christmas and
Winter wonderlands.

Who are we kidding about Mary's virginity?
Those Three Wise Men
Giving away priceless treasures
To some *street people's* baby
Were utter fools.

Night winds do not talk to little lambs;
But I spoke to Herod and told him
To kill all the boy babies.

My only hateful Hope
Is that Mankind will believe
In Santa Claus at Sears Roebuck—
Forget "Peace on Earth,"
Buy baubles at Bloomingdale's.

The best advise I ever gave
Was to Judas
About selling out the Nazarene;
Too cheaply,
I might add.

I cannot love;
Batteries not included.

THE KING OF SMILES

> "Oh villain, villain—smiling damnèd villain!. . .
> That one may smile, and smile, and be a villain."
> *Hamlet.*

He leads his troops to defend the coops,
To protect the towers and stiles.
He will kill, if pressed, and has killed the best
So, beware the King of Smiles.

In battle, hard-pressed, it was he who fought best:
Threw the enemy back for miles;
Ready and trim, for no contest too grim,
He endures as the King of Smiles.

The smile was not there when he was the heir
Of our old Lord, the King of Wiles;
Not a father's death, nor a spouse's theft
Could have made him the King of Smiles.

Only a friend, teaching fraud as an end,
Who is known as the Churl of Guiles,
Showed him how to deceive, make folks falsely believe
In our lord, the King of Smiles.

So, the smile carries on when true feelings are gone
And there's nothing now left for the files,
But a future of pains and the shallow remains
Of what reigns as our King of Smiles.

THE WILDERNESS TEMPTATION
(Matthew 4:1-11)

What misguided spirit
leads me into this wilderness?
Which weakness works against me next,
fatigue or hunger?
tell me, Father

You were so well pleased
with me
after my baptism
when we last spoke
but that was before
You let me get lost
and the tempter found me

so famished I could turn
stones to loaves
as the devil dares—
so fearful of falling
after he sets me on the pinnacle
and challenges me to fly—
so unworthy of all the kingdoms
and the glory in them,
knowing I lack the power

except through You
and that still, small voice
within me which roars,
Begone Satan!

for,
only *after* I have cast off
my own personal devils
will the angels
minister to me

DARK ANGEL

I.

Only when I almost lost him
Did I realize how much I loved him--
My identical twin brother, who went to the west coast,
While I stayed in Memphis.

In Palo Alto, brother bicycled everywhere;
Placing himself at the mercy of the world's worst drivers,
Including one steering a gravel truck,
Who side-swiped him and dragged him off his bicycle,
And under the truck's rear axle.

That was when the Dark Angel
Came to claim him.

II.

On a cool, mid-March Memphis morning
The call came from Stanford General Hospital.
The emergency room nurse's voice was sweet but sad,
"Your brother's been in an accident
His condition's critical—the doctors say
He has at best one chance in ten of living."

No! My mind screamed. Tears streamed down my cheeks
As I clenched my teeth and vowed, "He'll beat those odds."

Whatever it took, organ transplants included,
I was committed.

III.

Have you ever heard that irksome noise
Inside the back of your head
Where an insignificant word
Or phrase, or verse of bad poetry, or the lines
From some dumb song like "Achy-Breaky Heart"
Kept playing like a broken record on a drugstore jukebox?

I'd visited an elderly Jewish client
The night before the accident;
She'd worn a charm bracelet bearing
The Twelve Tribes of Israel,
One of which I hadn't previously noticed—ASHER.

As I spoke on the phone with the Stanford nurse,
That old mental mechanism began,
Whispering repeatedly, inside my head, "Asher."

At the time it meant nothing;
But days, then weeks of ASHER came and went,
While brother's life hung in the balance.

Then came the setback: Sepsis—
An infection in the blood that spread
Like God's curse in *Exodus* on the Egyptian firstborn,
Seeking to claim the elder twin;
Dangerously high fever drove the doctors to say
His time had come, and all the while the word "Asher""
Whispered away inside my head.

IV.

It was the Lenten season, when we Christians remember
Jesus' passion, death, and resurrection; His sacrifice for us;
But for me and my family, our sole prayer was
That my twin be spared.

On Easter morning,
The doctors declared the danger had passed;
Brother would recover,
And the echoes of Asher went out of my mind.

V.

My twin was moved to a private room with a telephone;
We spoke on our birthday.

"You nearly died," I said. "What was it like?
Was there a Tunnel of Light?
Did Grandma come to meet you?"

His already frail voice grew grim. "Nothing like that—
Different, dark, disturbing.
I was in a twilight world.
A Dark Angel had come for me.

"At first he looked human, almost beautiful,
But with wings blacker than printer's ink
And when I told him I chose Life,
He changed: growing big and ugly,
His hands became claws, cutting and tearing at my flesh;
I tried to run, but whichever way I went
He overtook me.

"Then I remembered, it was almost Easter
And called upon God, 'Lord, deliver me, I beseech you,
For You are everything, All-powerful,
And I am nothing without Your strength.
My soul belongs to You.'

"At that moment two Bright Angels appeared,
Bathed me in pure love,
And delivered me from the Dark Angel;
They came, they said, because I had chosen Life, and
Although I faced a difficult recovery,
My prayers, and of all those who loved me,
Were being answered;
It was God's will: Death held no dominion over me."

VI.

I'll never know what prompted me to ask the question,
"What was the name of the Dark Angel?"

The phone nearly fell from my hand
When my twin whispered the words,
"Asshur . . . Asshur-Baal."

LILITH ON THE MALL

lost cause, lost case—
good lawyers have bad days;
lunch time—I'm gone, out, anywhere

quick bite, cold day, hot chili
due for a dental checkup in twenty minutes
enough time for a leisurely walk
down Memphis' Mid-America Mall

and I wonder
who am I? where am I going?
why am I not a partner in the supergreat firm, yet?
why aren't my wife's legs thinner, her breasts larger?
why don't I have sons?

I don't recognize the pretty stranger at first
when she says, "hello"
she's changed—gray streaks in hair, some wrinkles,
but how could I forget
the smile
of my second best girl?

divorced after marrying on the rebound,
this ghost from college days and a thousand dreams
returns to haunt me—
she's available—with her thin legs and firm breasts,
her past boast to bear me sons,
but also the bad temper that drove her
to curse my impacted wisdom tooth
when I tried to use it for sympathy
after she caught me stepping out

I vowed then never to have it pulled
"I'm due at the dentist's," I tell her;
my tooth begins to ache again

"Don't you remember?" she asks

"Yes," I proclaim in pain, "and I've still got that tooth,"
(and my understanding wife and two precious daughters)
I'll keep them all —
thank you, Lord.

COLD GRAY THANKSGIVING DAY

On a cold gray Thanksgiving Day
down a brown dirt country road,
still stuffed from dinner, I walk with my wife
and my little Boston Terrier.

Behind, beside a warm wood fire,
almost grown, two teenage daughters
have no time except for television
and Tom Cruise,
so my mate, the icy wind, and Major Lee
accompany me.

My walking stick stands
between us and two cur dogs
who respect its danger,
but Major in his male delusion
thinks they have backed off
because of him.

It is one thing
to face and cope with
elements and animals in Nature;
yet another to deal with
human nature.

Making my living as a lawyer
killing other people's hopes and dreams,
trying to preserve those of my clients,
hoping one day to succeed
as a writer,
I wonder how much good
have I really done
protecting the illusions
of my loved ones?

DEBBIE'S WHITE CHRISTMAS

The gift of hurt
Keeps on giving:
Your last kindness
Consumed our Christmas Club account
Along with my whole week's wages.

At the hospital,
Where the expert medical staff
Repaired my face and your wrists,
They had nothing on hand
To mend hearts.

The emergency room specialist
Would not say that your alcohol
Was more powerful than his alcohol;
He had no drugs to counteract yours;
No feelings to fill the void of unfeeling
Caused from feeling too much,
Then forcing you
To dull that pain
With more substances.

As the intruding carolers
Inflicted "The First Noël" on families
Stranded in the Waiting Room,
I brought the car around
To pick you up
And drive us back
Through the snow flakes,
Wondering
What home have we to return to
So long as you seek solace
In white powder and amber liquids?

MORNING AT EAST ELEMENTARY SCHOOL

Separate but equal, holding hands,
On the schoolhouse steps they stand:
Two little girls—one black, one white—
Waiting for class to begin.

Equal now in the eyes of the law,
Equal as sisters in pain;
Poverty holds back either race,
But white makes it easy to gain.

They will grow up to find their place
Equal as sisters in pain:
Divided in race, divided in pace,
Divided families, divided in shame.

Little white girl will see the time
Her black friend won't come to play;
Little black girl will see the time
Her white friend will turn away.

Separate but equal, holding hands,
On the school house steps they stand:
Two little girls—one black, one white—
Waiting for class to begin.

TRAITOR

Mother took me,
Her sheltered son in short pants,
To kindergarten.

Left alone, I cried briefly,
Then asked Eddie Goldowski, the biggest boy there,
If I could join his play group.

Eddie laughed at me,
Pushed me down, and called me a sissy;
He also said bad things about my mother.

No choice, no issue;
Just whip Eddie
In a fair fight to show his followers
What a true leader was.

So sure of victory; such vain aspirations.

Two black eyes later,
This little warrior,
Still undaunted,
Took a big toy wooden block
And smacked the stinkiness out of Eddie.

His nose bled forever.

We were sent to the Principal's office
To see Miss Stanton—
250 pounds of repressed hatred
In a cheap blue rayon dress.

Pretending propriety, masking her seethings
Beneath the sweet smell of Chanel No. 5,
Ever-smiling Miss Stanton taught Eddie and me
With six hard raps from a wooden ruler
About the evils of resorting to violence.

Agreeing that I was sorry,
Mother came to take me home and, once inside our car,

I protested that I had done this in her defense
And Miss Stanton was a GROSS FAT PIG.

In shock, she dragged me
And my still-hurting bottom
Once more before Miss Stanton
To confess and apologize for calling that lady
A GROSS FAT PIG behind her back:
Thereby sentencing me to six years
At hard labor.

FACING THE FEAR

"The key to courage," my father told me,
"Is facing your fear. That's what heroes do—
 Cowards run away."

I watched Dad face his fear from the time I was six,
When the doctor told Mother
The lump on Dad's neck was a lymph node;
Cancer had invaded and spread;
Her only consolation could be that it moved slowly;
Surgery, radiation treatments, and chemo-therapy were options;
She had six months to six years before widowhood.

The only word the doctor told Dad was "Hodgkins."
He caught the meaning.
Knowing each day was grace, Dad lasted eleven years.
They weren't all happy, but they were his.

He could have quit after Grandmother died,
Could have spent his inheritance on mindless pursuits,
Could have left Mother and us for one final party,
Could have arranged a hunting accident or an overdose
 of tranquilizers when the pain became almost unbearable,
Could have sought exotic "miracle" cures at exorbitant prices,
But chose instead because he loved his family
To face his fear.

He told Death, "Come for me when you're ready,
But I'm not waiting around for you." And he meant it.

He could have claimed disability,
Could have collected a pension,
Could have turned his face to the wall and stayed in bed.
He didn't.

Instead, he completed college and earned his degree,
Built a wing and two additions to our home,
Raised three sons almost to manhood,
Saw his marriage last through its twentieth anniversary,

Taught school
Until two weeks before he died,
Until cancer twisted around his spine and wouldn't let him
walk,
Until Death grew serious about taking him.

Dad's courage showed in his facing Life
With all the doubts and fears that accompany it.
Having mastered Life,
Dad faced Death like a hero.

UH-OH!

Subpoenaed by Sub-committee
Bill Clinton said, "Oh, no—not me,
Nor my innocent daughter
Was involved in *Whitewater*—
But, maybe . . . perhaps . . . Hillary?"

SHOW ME THE WAY

Show me the way, Wendy,
Back from Never-Never Land;
I know I can't go on
Fighting pirates, inciting Indians,
Hanging out with the Lost Boys;
Everyone says I must grow up.

But why, Wendy,
If it means I can't fly anymore?

Isn't there always supposed to be somebody else
Out there to pick up the tab?
Daddy, Mamma, Aunt Ruth?
Not me.

For I can stay
Cute, witty, clever, and pretty
Forever
In a world where good guys always win.

Where are the good guys, Wendy?
Am I all that's left?

Why am I faced with
      Mortgage payments,
            Insurance premiums,
                  Taxes and utilities?

Why won't your love
Take care of those things, Wendy?
If your love is so strong, why won't it stop
      My hair from thinning and
           My teeth from falling out?

Your love is no good for me, Wendy,
If I can't stay young forever.

I'm catching the next pirate ship and sailing
Back over the Moon and
Beyond the North Star, Wendy,
Where I can harass Ol' Cap'n Hook to my heart's content
And frolic with Tinkerbell and Princess Tiger Lily.

You can have the house, Wendy,
Plus the car and make the payments, too;
Let the lawyers
Figure it all out.

THE VOID

Winter solstice—
Short gray days;
Long tenebrous nights;
Darkness reigns:
The Void.

Spring's hope,
Summer's cheer,
Autumn's harvest—
All succumb to
The Void.

The Old Year dies.

But then,
Days lengthen;
Within a week
A Child is born
And a Star
Appears in the East.

The New Year comes.

Hope,
Peace,
God's promise;
New Light,
Love
To fill
The Void.

PAULIE THE PARROT

Paulie the parrot lived content inside his cage
In a San Francisco pet shop, until the widow Gage
Saw him through the store window and bought him,
Unaware of what bad manners someone else had taught him.

When they arrived at her mansion high up on Nob Hill,
Those elegant trappings he saw gave him quite a thrill—
Marble tile, oriental rugs, crystal everywhere—
Such sights drove Paulie in a frenzy to declare:
"My, oh my, feed me cheese just like a mouse,
But, sweet Jesus, lady, you have such a fancy house!"

In shock, the widow Gage brusquely told her bird,
"This place is a Christian home, I'm stunned at what I heard;
To cure you of such speech I think that I shall park
You in the downstairs closet where it's very, very dark."

And so, for half an hour's time, the prissy widow Gage
Left Paulie in the darkness, perched inside his cage;
Hoping he'd learned his lesson, she finally brought him out
And took him to the dining room, to show him all about—
Irish linens, wedgewood china, polished silver
                                               everywhere—
Such sights drove Paulie in a frenzy to declare:
"My, oh my, feed me cheese just like a mouse,
But, sweet Jesus, lady, you have such a fancy house!"

In shock, the widow Gage brusquely told her bird,
"This place is a Christian home, I'm stunned at what I heard;
I warned you not to use such speech, so now I think I'll
                                               park
You inside the icebox where it's *cold* as well as dark."

Within the refrigerator, Paulie's beak began to chatter
His eyes adjusted as he looked down upon a platter
Where next to him, half-carved, a Christmas turkey lay—
"Good Lord! Cousin," he exclaimed, "whatever did *you*
                                                    say?"

GARFIELD'S GUT

Jon asked his pet Garfield the Cat,
"Why are you so terribly fat?"
Garf said, "Fish is fine
And chicken divine;
But *lasagna's* what's made me like that!"

INTO THE LIGHT

When I was four, I spent a quarter, my entire fortune,
On a Nutty Buddy,
The biggest treat the ice cream vendor had—
Vanilla, stuffed in a sugar cone,
Topped with chocolate fudge and chopped nuts;
My little girl taste buds sang
The Hallelujah Chorus in perfect harmony
As I laved my tongue
Over the cold brown crunchy sweetness.

Momentarily I forgot about
July's sweltering heat in pre-airconditioned Memphis
Until I tilted the cone for a better lick
And its delicious, gooey contents dropped to the sidewalk
With a heart-breaking splat.

Frankie, my nursemaid, sipping icewater,
Watched me burst into tears.
She set down her glass,
Swept me up in her strong brown arms, and said,
"Hush, child. Cryin' ain't gonna fix nuthin'."

When she wiped my damp cheeks dry, I asked,
"Where do tears go?"

She held the wet white handkerchief up in the sunlight,
Where it quickly dried.
"Into the light and back to God."

When I was sixteen, my first real boyfriend
Asked Cindy Lou Saunders, the prettiest girl in our class
To go with him to the Homecoming Dance instead of me.
Thinking I was surely going to die,
I took to my bedroom and buried my face in my pillow.
Frankie came to comfort me, once more saying,
"Hush, child. Cryin' ain't gonna fix nuthin'."
She wiped the tears from my face
And held the wet white hanky up to dry in the sunlight.

"See," she reassured me,
"Into the light and back to God."

Losing my parents and my dear wise maid,
The tears have fallen and dried.
Though I remember her admonition,
The weeping still comes with each loss.

The hardest time I ever had
Was when my husband died.
But I take my comfort in knowing,
Like tears, a soul must go
Into the light and back to God.

AFTER THE "WILDING"
(A villanelle for the Central Park Jogger—April 20, 1989)

A spark went out in Central Park last night,
One soul who faced life unafraid—
She fought the Darkness, striving for the Light.

In one mad moment, beyond hope of flight,
She was captured by the wilding horde—
A spark went out in Central Park last night.

She pled the hoodlums to excuse her plight,
Hoping monsters could have pity on a maid;
She fought the Darkness, striving for the Light.

But God turned his head, and shut his sight;
Even her Guardian Angel fled—
A spark went out in Central Park last night.

Some Samaritan found the wounded sprite;
Family, friends, physicians wept and prayed—
She fought the Darkness, striving for the Light.

May she be healed, to work again for Right;
May blind Justice see her tormentors repaid.
A spark went out in Central Park last night—
She fought the Darkness, striving for the Light.

SUMMER STORM

Memphis in July—Saturday—hot and dry,
Great day to take kids to the pool,
Soak up sun and tan,
Read bulletins for the work week ahead—
Even daddies can be kids again, temporarily.

Cool water relieves heat and frustration
As all problems from the office
Momentarily disappear, until

Thunderheads rumble across the sky like Hell's Angels,
Blotting out the sun, threatening weekend recreation;
Lifeguard yells, "Lightning! Everyone out of the water."

Rain plummets in pitchforks
No room left under the shelter of the oak-shadowed gazebo
Now filled with cold, damp, swimsuited bodies
Scrambling for towels in short supply.

Huddling over hot dogs and Cokes,
The little ones' questions begin:
"When will the rain stop, Daddy?"
"Why is it thundering?"
"Is Mother Nature mad?"

Like Lear on the heath, I struggle for answers.

Winds gust to gale force—
The small building dwarfed by the immense oak
No longer seems secure;
Danger is clear and present.

Raindrops blast us, blown sideways by cruel breezes—
The great tree groans—sinister creaking noises;
"Come on, children," I shout, bullying out of love and fear,
"Follow me—NOW!"

Seconds later, breathless, but safe
Inside our brick clubhouse,
We watch the oak topple, taking the gazebo with it.

THE DAY I MET THE FAMOUS WRITER AT THE ROUND TABLE BOOKSTORE

awakening
from the Land of Dreamy Dreams
she must find reality
painful

it's so okay
to come and buy her books
but
don't ask Questions.

Shop Talk
is not to be shared with
unpublished novelists

especially since she
never had to struggle
but, like Athena, burst full blown
upon the literary scene
(also already a goddess —
at least in her own mind)

she was INVITED
to be published

Do Tell!

more than a
Little Brown'd off
I return
my autographed edition,
which
I Cannot Get Far Enough Away,
to the sales clerk
And demand a full refund

delighted to breathe
Garlic
At a literary
Vampire.

GHIA'S LESSON

Like an Oriental potentate surveying his palatinate
Sleek, coal black Ghia lies atop the kitchen counter
"Shoo, cat!" I say. "You know you can't stay *there*."

Flicking his tail, he squints green eyes at me,
Not budging—he knows I'm only a visitor.

"Who do you think you are?" I ask.
"Me…" he answers. Not "Meow," but "Me."
He's staked out his domain at my in-laws' home.

"Would you like me to rub your back, your Majesty?"
Immediately he's purring, eyes closed, one white whisker
Curls upward, like the tusk on a rogue elephant;
My rub progresses—behind his ears, beneath his throat,
His purring resounds, rivalling the rumbling
Of the refrigerator's motor.

But, when I move to rub his tummy,
Without warning, he attacks—
Four sets of claws, upper and lower fangs,
All descend in orchestrated agony
Upon my unsuspecting hand.

Those who know cats swear that's only being playful;
My punctured flesh and broken blood vessels do not agree.

Wrenching my wounded hand away, I stare at Ghia.
Proudly meeting my gaze, his eyes betray delight.
"Gotcha!" they say.
He's smiling. Lucifer from Disney's *Cinderella*.
This is no dumb animal.

My tomboy daughter's Superblaster squirtgun
Lies on a nearby chair.
With six staccato bursts, I open up on Ghia.
"Ow! Ow! Ow! Ow!Ow! Ow!"
The big, bad black kitty shrieks,
Running around the kitchen.
No "Me's" this time.

"What's the matter?" my mother-in-law asks.
"Nothing," I lie.
On my next day's visit, Ghia lets me rub his tummy and Purrs, promising (perhaps) no more surprises.

MELVIN'S MESSAGE

"Everythin' gonna be all right,"
Tuxedoed Melvin used to say
From his post as our head waiter
At the country club each day.

Sparkling teeth and flashing eyes,
Black skin like a high-buffed shoe;
Makin' folks feel welcome
Was what he best could do.

Didn't matter if your day went bad,
If you came to the club at night,
When Mel saw you, he'd smile and say,
"Everythin' gonna be all right!"

Seems the club had problems—
Dues went up and folks got tired
Of paying for his services—
Its Board had Melvin fired.

We'd see him in his old street clothes—
Drunk, downtown at night;
He'd smile, accept our tips, and say,
"Everythin' gonna be all right."

Last week we buried Mel;
In his tux he made quite a sight;
At the wake, we all remembered,
"Everythin' gonna be all right!"

REUNION REFLECTION
(CLASS OF '71)

Light years ago our worlds collided
Scorching the heavens with their sparks;
Adonis had found his Venus
And all the Titans trembled.

Then the earth cooled
And crusted over;
Leaving only the lava
Boiling below.

Now you reappear,
Fat husband, whining children in tow and
Flash me the briefest of smiles—
Whether they shine with love or hate,
Your eyes say you still care,
The allure is still there.

Considering the depth of the crater
Left by your extinct volcano,
I wonder what it would be worth
To make you erupt again?

ESAU REMEMBERS
(Genesis 33)

You learned to cheat,
My smooth brother,
Even before you strove with God and men—
Deceived me into bartering my birthright
For a cheap lunch.

Then, hating my hairiness
You assumed it to receive
Our father's
Blessing.

Fearing my wrath
You fled
To the East,
Married the daughters of Laban,
And grew rich.

Returning,
You seek peace.

Groveling on the ground
Before me,
Attempting bribes
With sheep and cattle;
Do you really think
I have forgotten
The Curse?

We embrace at present,
Postponing
For three or more
Millenia
Edom's revenge.

TO WINIFRED FOR "PEPE" AND "NITRO"
(Her Boston Terriers)

Ugly little pouting smashed-in faces
glaring back in black-and-white indignation;
they look guilty because they are.
But don't expect contrition—
at best you'll get a stare
from a pair of cocked heads
like you have"t got half-good sense
if you believe they did not chew up
your antique tapestry.

After all, it is common knowledge
that, after God made
all the other dogs—
all those high-falutin'
high class, high-strung other dogs,
He used the leftover scraps
to make the Boston Terriers;
what with those little Hitler
moustaches and maroon bug-eyes
not even a mother could love
them too much, unless she
herself happened to own one.

Also remember that your bed,
where they sleep like secure sailors
shaking the rafters with their snorings,
no longer belongs to you—
they took it for their own
by guile and force of arms,
by manifest destiny.

Barking at odd hours,
barking to get your attention,
barking to remind you really
who is master and who must serve

(they will not bite unless
they need to make a point),
there is still some comfort
in the ultimate knowledge that,
outside the home they
would be utterly helpless.

CASSIE'S CURSE

From Memphis through a snowstorm
Last March I drove up to Saint Lou;
With no way to suspect then
What Al's pet cat would do.

We read our poems at the coffee house;
Al let me have his bedroom;
Cassie hissed and spat at me
And plotted my Rockport's doom.

Al, you were a gracious host—
Lots of fun in old Saint Lou-—
But Goddamn Cassie to Cat Hell
For SPRAYING in my shoe!

HAIKU

crabgrass creeps across
earth stripped by human toxins
Nature recovers

WAITING ON A WET BALCONY

Waiting on a wet balcony
Watching rain fall
Lightning arcs, threatening —
Thunder follows
Night air fills with sweetness
Making your memory more painful

Then:
Huddling
Naked on the carpet
Just inside, just off the balcony
While the rain fell
We enjoyed
A more delicious
Wetness

Smoke swirling from twin cigarettes
Brandy in our snifters
Languished while we
Consumed each other

Two stars went nova
Simultaneously

Dual dark solar systems
Left in the aftermath

Now:
Wishing upon your dark star
Praying for your return
I remember
Your promise of
Forever

Doomed
Like all mortal
Commitments

CONSOLATION PRIZE

The innocent white envelope
Belies
Black disappointments
Inside:

As the winners' names
Are called,
Mine
Is not included.

The only sure reward
For song
Is the joy
Of singing.

ADIEU

Your kiss lingered on my
 lips like the fragrance of
   freshly crushed rose petals.
I knew then it would be

   . The last time I saw you.
    The last time I saw you

 you hinted the garden
held more roses to pluck,
  but thorns had grown up thick,
choking your Prince Charming.

CREDITS

"Recovering My Sanity" won a Second Place Award in the 1994 Mid-South Poetry Festival, Memphis, TN.

"Bedazzled" won a Second Place Award in the 1993 Mid-South Poetry Festival, Memphis, TN.

"Response" won a Third Place in the Mississippi Poetry Society 1995 Annual Contest and was published in the 1995 *Mississippi Poetry Journal.*

"Forever Friends" was published in the April, 1995 edition of *Tradition* (Little Rock, AR).

"Last October" won an Honorable Mention in the 1994 Mid-South Poetry Festival, Memphis, Tennessee, and was included in *Our Time Is Limited* (Zapizdat Publications: Palo Alto, CA; 1994).

"The Psychiatrist's Patients' Pet Peeves" won an Honorable Mention at the 1995 Arkansas Writers' Conference, Little Rock, AR.

"Grandpa Frank and His Bostons" won Third Place in the Grand Prize Category in the Mississippi Poetry Society 1994 Annual Contest and was published in the 1994 *Mississippi Poetry Journal.*

"Resolution" appeared in *The Visitation of Dionysius* (Plowman Press: Whitby, Ontario; 1989) and in *Generations* (Zapizdat Publications: Palo Alto, CA; 1993).

"Custer's Mistress" won an Honorable Mention in the Native American Poetry Category (Oklahoma) at the 1994 National Federation of State Poetry Societies Convention and was included in *Our Time Is Limited* (Zapizdat Publications: Palo Alto, CA; 1994).

"Vampyr" appeared in the July, 1993 issue of *Realm of the Vampire* (Full Moon Publications: Metaire, LA).

"To Lady" appeared in the Fall 1992 issue of *Writers on the River* (Mid-South Writers Assoc.: Memphis, TN).

"Blanche Cole" won First Place in the Spoon River Category at the 1992 Mid-South Poetry Festival, Memphis, TN and was published in *Tennessee Voices*, 1993 (Poetry Society of Tennessee).

"The King of Smiles" appeared in *The Visitation of Dionysius* (Plowman Press: Whitby, Ontario; 1989).

"Dark Angel" won an Honorable Mention in the Grand Prize Category in the Mississippi Poetry Society 1995 Annual Contest and was published in the 1995 *Mississippi Poetry Journal*.

"Cold Gray Thanksgiving Day" won Second Place in the PST November, 1993 Monthly Contest and was published in *Tennessee Voices*, 1994 (Poetry Society of Tennessee).

"Debbie's White Christmas" won Third Place in the Free Verse Category at the 1989 Ozark Creative Writers' Conference (Eureka Springs, AR) and won Honorable Mentions in both the Grandmother Earth 1994 Contest and the Iliad Press 1994 National Competition.

"Morning at East Elementary School" appeared in *The Visitation of Dionysius* (Plowman Press: Whitby, Ontario; 1989) and also appeared in a Plowman Press anthology bearing its name as the title poem in 1990.

"Traitor" won Third Place in the Narrative Poem category in the Mississippi Writers' Guild 1993 Annual Contest and Honorable Mention in the Grand Prize Category at the 1990 Ozark Creative Writers' Conference.

"Facing the Fear" won an Honorable Mention in the 1995 Mid-South Poetry Festival, Memphis, TN.

"Uh-Oh!" won Third Place in the 1994 Mid-South Writers' Conference, Memphis, TN, and was published in the Spring 1995 issue of *Writers on the River* (Mid-South Writers Assoc.: Memphis, TN).

"The Void" won Second Place in the PST January, 1994 Monthly Contest and was published in *Tennessee Voices*, 1994 (Poetry Society of Tennessee). It also was a finalist in the 1994 Southern Poetry Competition and was included in *Voices of the South* (Pass Christian, MS; 1994).

"Paulie the Parrot" won an Honorable Mention in the 1995 Mid-South Writers' Conference, Memphis, TN,

"Garfield's Gut" was included in *Into the Limerick Grove* (Zapizdat Publications: Palo Alto, CA; 1993).

"Into the Light" won Third Place in the 1995 Mid-South Poetry Festival, Memphis, TN.

"After the Wilding" appeared in *The Visitation of Dionysius* (Plowman Press: Whitby, Ontario; 1989).

"Summer Storm" won Third Place in the PST April, 1995 Monthly Contest.

"Ghia's Lesson" won Third Place in the PST November, 1995 Monthly Contest.

"Melvin's Message" appeared in the December 1993, edition of *Tradition* (op. cit.).

"Esau Remembers" won a Second Place Award at the 1991 Ozark Creative Writers' Conference.

"To Winifred for 'Pepe' and 'Nitro'" was published in the Winter 1990 edition of *Pet Gazette* (Daytona Beach, FL).

"Cassie's Curse" was disqualified from a First Place Award in the 1993 Mid-South Poetry Festival for offending the sponsor-judge by "taking the Lord's name in vain." The poet was unaware that the Ten Commandments were incorporated into the contest rules.

"Haiku" won a Third Place at the 1991 Ozark Creative Writers' Conference.

"Waiting on a Wet Balcony" won an Honorable Mention in the 1993 Mid-South Poetry Festival.

"Adieu" won Third Place in the PST December, 1995 Monthly Contest.

A Prieview: Three Stories from

MONSTERS FROM MEMPHIS

By Beecher Smith

THE BURROWER
FROM THE BLUFF

April 19: dusk

    This note pad you brought me, Bailey Stratton—your small charity to an apparent madman—may be my only chance to communicate. Perhaps I can convince you these aren't the ravings of a lunatic.
    I pray I can complete this, and persuade you to release me before *Dhumin* finds me. Eventually he will. Just like he found Pitt and Tarterro.
    Trying to tell you about it in person seemed so useless. Oh, you tried to look interested. But you forgot you were talking to another lawyer. I saw when your eyes glazed over.
    Did you think you were fooling me—Snyder Trask? Hell, I was trying lawsuits when you were soiling your diapers. I've forgotten more body language than you'll ever learn. Wait. I'm sorry. Not smart, when you're helping me. It's the strain.
    I may crack up—but not yet.
    When I tried to talk to you, I couldn't quit stammering. *He* probably caused that, too. But I *can* write legibly, even though my hand shakes pretty bad. You must read this—please!
    I— — — — — — — — —
    See how my script jumped? That was an earthquake *tremor*. But not a normal one. No tectonic shifts. Dhumin at work. It's only a matter of time before he finds me, even here!
    Bailey, you have to move me.

April 20: just before dawn

    The floor nurse ordered me sedated last night. I hid this pad before they came. You, Bailey, my court appointed guardian, are my only hope! Read this objectively. I AM NOT MAD!
    I'll start at the beginning:

After 35 years I had one of the best practices in Memphis. My client list included a major bank, three insurance companies, several national corporations. All paid me handsome regular retainers.

But, as sometime happens, my personal and family's spending outdistanced my earning capacity. I was facing bankruptcy. To my wife and children, our summer home on Nantucket, yacht, buying trips to New York and Paris, three country club memberships, and servants were *necessities*, not luxuries.

I had made some wise investments, which sustained our high lifestyle. When the markets dropped, I almost lost everything.

My own bank turned on me first. I had creditors lined up in the lobby of my firm, all wanting to know when they would be paid. I was good at stalling them—coaxing, cajoling, even lying— but none of those tactics would work for long.

Then Pitt and Tarterro showed up.

You remember them, don't you? Pitt, the ivy leaguer, who came from old Memphis money. Tarterro's cash was new and not clean.

Anyway, they appeared at my office one gray afternoon last February, about two weeks after my financial troubles started. Henry Pitt breezed through the doorway, gave me a warm, firm grip, then moved aside for Tarterro to shake my hand.

Bedecked with a white, lapel carnation on his dark blue, worsted wool, custom-tailored suit and sporting a regimental blue-and-red striped tie, Pitt appeared impeccably dressed. Especially when compared to his short, heavyset colleague, who wore a green-and-brown checked wool blend winter sport coat, bright yellow slacks, and a hand-painted sienna necktie that looked like roadkill.

"Thanks for seeing us," Pitt opened. "Word has gotten around you could use some new clients."

"Yeah," Ronnie chimed in with a hoarse, gritty voice, "who will pay well because you are influential and respectable."

My senses went on guard immediately. Coming from Tarterro, an offer to purchase my services sounded like the solicitation of a prostitute.

"What do you want from me?" I asked.

"It's a simple case," Pitt replied. "We lost before the zoning board and need you to appeal to the City Council."

I remembered the matter. "Isn't this about the Indian mounds on the bluff, overlooking the river? The City is broke and must raise cash. You must obtain a favorable rezoning to put up a condo development."

"Yeah. Dat's us," Tarterro answered.

I wondered how anybody with such atrocious diction could have finished engineering school. "Wasn't there a big issue about the mounds being sacred to the Indians—some Constitutional prohibition against disturbing those ancient landmarks?"

"Quite correct, sport," Pitt responded.

"What makes you think *I* could turn this thing around?"

Tarterro grinned, displaying two gold caps on his front teeth. "You're a talented attorney, Mr. Trask. We seen you win appeals after other lawyers—pardon the expression—screw up. You can convince the City Council."

"But, Mr. Tarterro, your case doesn't offer much promise."

Tarterro winked at Pitt, who said, "Look, Snyder, we know you're in some *temporary financial difficulty*."

I despised how he turned those upper class, old school phrases. He motioned toward the black, lizard skin briefcase Tarterro clutched, and added, "We thought a *small retainer* might convince you as to the righteousness of our cause."

At that, Tarterro opened the case, revealing neatly stacked rows of crisp, new $100 bills.

"Count it," Pitt assured, "and you'll find $100,000, none of which needs to be reported."

"But that's i-illegal," I stammered, a bad habit you've seen me exhibit under pressure, Bailey.

"Don't worry, Mr. Trask," Tarterro responded. "You're much better off not having to pay tax. We won't mind not claiming the deduction. Everybody's happy, right?"

I knew then that their "principals" weren't legitimate businessmen. But, if I didn't accept their money my credit would soon be ruined. I let myself be bought.

Oh God! *Another tremor*. Louder, longer, and closer. How much time do I have?

I gave their case my complete attention. My staff researched the state and federal laws. One of my brightest and best, a kid two years out of Vanderbilt, found a loophole.

In the National Historical Landmark legislation there was no reference to those particular Indian mounds. The state laws prohibited them from being destroyed. Nothing indicated they couldn't be *moved*—just like white men had moved the red men who built them.

When I informed Pitt he chuckled. "That's simply *capital*, old sport. My principals can easily find another site for those. They can't find another location for riverfront development. Millions are involved."

I drafted the appeal, convinced my clients' willingness to "preserve the landmarks" should satisfy the Council.

The day before the hearing I had another unexpected visitor. It was after five. The electronic security bell indicated someone had come in. In the office lobby, I saw a dirty looking, brown skinned old man in tattered overalls. He wore his iron gray hair long, with a single tight braid on each shoulder. His clothes and scuffed black work boots gave off faint traces of barnyard odors.

He said, in a throaty voice, "I need to see Mr. Snyder Trask."

"That's me. But I'm headed home. If you want an appointment, you'll have to call my secretary in the morning."

His stare arrested me. In a voice so cold and resolute it could have frozen water, he announced, "I am Chief Russell Two Bears. *You need to see me.*"

Some preternatural force made me stay and listen.

He said, "There is a hearing tomorrow. You plan to ask the city fathers for permission to move my people's sacred mounds. *You must not do this.*"

I tried to remain courteous. "Look, Chief I'm their lawyer. If your people don't like it, hire an attorney. Don't expect me to drop a paying client on account of any sob stories you might tell me the day before—"

He rose indignantly. "I came, Mr. Trask," he said slowly, in a tone of controlled emotion, "to warn that you are dealing with forces beyond your control. A very GREAT EVIL will consume you if you are not careful."

Oh Lord, I thought, *does even this stinking old Indian know I've been bought by the mob?* But to my surprise he cautioned against an entirely different kind of malevolence, asking, in a trembling voice, "You no doubt have never heard of the *Uktena?*"

I laughed nervously. "No."

"Then I shall inform you. It might change your mind.

"Before the coming of the white man, even before the red man, this earth was ruled by an evil race known as the Great Old Ones. Most were banished back to the stars from whence they came by the Elder Gods under *Wakàn Tanka*, the Great Spirit. Some eluded banishment and remained to wreak terror on my ancestors."

Trying to humor him into leaving, I said, "Well, that's all very interesting, but I don't see what that has to do with my law practice."

His eyes grew steely, his voice tense. "They remain a threat today. One especially. You make it so."

"How?"

"Cherokee, Choctaw, and Chickasaw legends tell of the Uktena, a great snake that comes from the underworld. It has antlers like a deer and wings like an eagle. It inhabits the deep waters, high places, and caverns beneath the earth. It can bore like a giant earthworm and travels freely between the land of the living and that of the dead. Sometimes it seeks souls to take back to the lower depths.

"The Uktena comes out only at night. Dwelling mostly underground, it shuns the sun and all bright light. But it can be active during the day, so long as it remains in darkness.

"Ages ago, long before the white man arrived, the most terrible of all the Uktena—*Dhumin*—dwelled beneath where Memphis stands today. Its tunneling through layers of bedrock caused the formation of the wonderful water reservoir below this city. The god's underground activities also may have created the New Madrid fault, source of many earthquake fears.

"As long as it left our people alone, they worshiped it with awe and reverence. But when it began attacking randomly at night, after several families and even some whole clans disappeared, all the tribes in the region united against it. By using fire, the only thing Dhumin fears, thousands of braves carrying torches encircled him and forced him to tunnel underneath the bluff, to where the rock was so hard and thick that he became trapped."

"Why are you telling me this?" I interrupted.

"It is no legend. Dhumin sleeps deep beneath those mounds. My forefathers invoked a curse: Dhumin will destroy whoever disturbs him."

All of this I silently dismissed as primitive tribal gibberish. I politely advised the Chief I would consider his warning.

What kind of lawyer would be swayed by such claptrap? I told Pitt and Tarterro the next morning. Both of them thought it was hysterically funny—a real knee-slapper. Alas, had we heeded, they would still be alive and I would not be terrified.

I hear the nurse coming down the hall. It's quitting time again. I'm almost through, Bailey.

April 21: early morning before sunrise

Another tremor awoke me. Two ceiling tiles fell. He's close. Please come, Bailey. I know you will, but ten o'clock seems a month away.

You already know I didn't exactly breeze through the appeal. It passed by one vote. Rumors soon circulated that the council member casting the deciding ballot had been bribed.

A month later, local and national media sucked up the story about the "terrible accident," when Tarterro's crew attempted to move the mounds. They said heavy equipment, rolling over an undetected subterranean cavern, caused a cave-in. Tarterro and eight crew members disappeared. What happened to their bodies?

I tried in vain to locate the Chief. Supposedly he left for Oklahoma the day after the hearing.

The morning after Tarterro's "accident," when Pitt was leaving for work, he started his car and the pavement collapsed. He and his automobile sank from sight. A defective sewer? Hardly.

What about the councilman who cast the swing vote? He's vanished! There's a huge hole in his back yard.

Are these coincidences? At each "accident site" the police found, covered with human blood, oblong disks the size of dinner plates—the scales of a giant reptile!

Now you understand, Bailey, why I developed a case of "nerves" when a wing of my home collapsed. Thank God I had just pulled into the driveway and my family was out of town.

My doctor had no right to commit me. Surely you must now agree?

Damn! Another tremor. More falling ceiling tiles. This building—it's five stories tall and each floor is built of steel and reinforced concrete.

Oh Lord. The whole structure is shuddering. A damn giant snake can't be *that powerful*. Somebody could stop it with fire, bury it again like the Indians did.

I can hardly write with the floor and walls trembling.

But the lights are on in the building, and shining bright. According to the legend, Dhumin hates light. So I guess I'm safe.

Bailey, where are you?

Jesus Christ! The lights just went out. Only those dim amber emergency lamps remain on.

Now I hear it—something slithering—huge, horrible—forcing its way up the elevator shaft.

Get me out before it's too lat

NOTE: The *Uktena* is an authentic native American legend of the Southeastern tribes.

DUE PROCESS

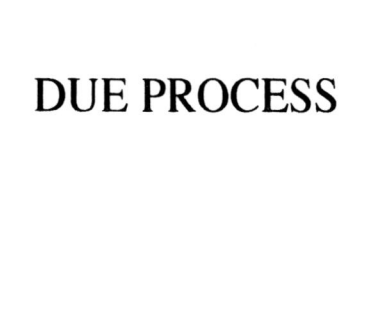

I saw what happened to Izzie, Captain Mitchell. Public defender says I can talk, now that you've agreed not to prosecute. Izzie didn't just disappear.

But I didn't murder him. He was *taken*. Don't go thinkin' me crazy. I can explain. Yeah. Thanks. I would like a cigarette.

Here's how it went.

Izzie decides to retire. Wants to move to Florida. I make a decent living as a private investigator, myself, but Izzie Glassman was the *best*. He offers to sell me his business at a good price with reasonable terms, so I accept. It was a handshake deal. He was to get a share of the income for the next five years.

No, he wasn't what you'd call a friend. Nobody really *liked* Izzie. He was so intense. You know, Captain, how he'd come up behind you and shout your name in that shrill, loud voice of his—make you jump—like it was a big joke? He expected you to laugh, but nobody ever did.

We all know the man made people uncomfortable. His appearance didn't help. Remember his low forehead and how hairy he was? He might have passed for an ape. His coal-black eyes were little and set too close together, but they burned all the time.

You recall how his nose was large and laced with broken blood vessels that gave it a purple hue? Heavy drinkin' does that to folks, don't it?

We all got the impression he was mad at the world because his parents were poor. Well, believe me, it was also obvious he had set out long ago to better his lot. Remember the $500 suits he wore and the diamond solitaire pinkie ring he sported? They would have been the envy of a mafia don!

The man had no social skills. He never helped anybody unless there was something in it for him. But you know all that, Captain Mitchell.

He was showing me that afternoon how he handled things—everybody's got his own style, you know. I'd already given him a downpayment and signed the papers. He was fulfilling his part of the bargain. That's what we were doing together two days before Christmas. Izzie already had his plane ticket for Florida to fly down on

Christmas Eve to be with his family, even though it was not a religious holiday for him.

Izzie's biggest business was finding people who dodge regular process servers. When folks owe money or won't pay their rent, they have to be found and given official court papers telling them they've been sued. If a creditor can't find them, he can't collect. Even a deadbeat tenant can't be evicted without notice. You know, Captain, it's called "due process."

I thought I knew some pretty dirty tricks, but nobody was better than Izzie. When a debtor wouldn't claim a registered letter, Izzie would find his unlisted phone number, call him, and tell him he'd won the sweepstakes. After the poor schmuck goes to the post office and signs the receipt he finds out he's been served papers to appear in court.

That last afternoon we were together, after we finished going over his accounts and receivables balance, he shows me one of his really great stunts. One of his best clients and our city's biggest slumlord has a tenement he wants to tear down. There was one renter left, a little old lady, who refused to leave. When the Sheriff's deputy tried to serve eviction papers on her, she wouldn't come to the door. He'd returned the papers as "not to be found." The landlord hired Izzie.

In the darkened, unheated hall of that rat-infested apartment building, Izzie rolls up a newspaper and strikes a match. He touches the flame to the paper and points the roll downward, causing the flame to climb and smoke to billow. He drops the paper torch into a tin bucket and shoves it against the door to the lady's apartment. Giving me a wicked wink, he yells, "Fire! Fire! Everybody out."

The elderly lady appears at the door wearing a topcoat over a dressing gown. Her face shows she's scared pretty bad, only to turn real angry when she sees the smoke coming out of the pail.

"Greetings, Mrs. Johnston," Izzie says with a smile like he's doin' her a big favor when he hands her the eviction notice.

She gives him and me both a scowl so sour it could curdle cream and says, "Damn you. Haven't you got anything better to do than trick a poor widow?"

Izzie shrugs. "Just my job. But I'm paid to do it.'"

He leads me out into the cold drizzle. He says, "That's

84

about all for now. Why don't you buy me a beer? There's a bar on the next block."

I'm ready to get out of the chill, even if I have to buy the drinks. We duck into a dive on Madison Avenue. It only serves beer, so I order two Michelob drafts.

That's when we see this black dude wearin' the wildest outfit—a three-piece dark gray suit, a red silk shirt, white necktie, and a black cape with red satin lining. Has on a wide-brimmed dark felt hat. He's sporting a moustache and goatee. Looks real cultured, like some actor or college professor. I'm thinking, *probably some pimp or a queer—midtown Memphis is full of both nowadays*. He's sittin' at the bar by himself, real polite-like, minding his own business.

Izzie asks me for a cigarette and I tap one out of my pack for him. But I'm out of matches and Izzie's lighter don't work. So we ask the dude, "Got a light?"

Funny thing. He touches his index finger once to the ends of both our cigs and—Presto—they're lit! Neat trick.

"How'd you do that?" I ask.

He smiles and shrugs. "Magic," he says.

"Are you a magician?" I ask.

"No," he says. "My name is Mephisto. I am a *Summoner*."

"You serve summonses?" Izzie asks. "We do that. Are you a private dick, too?"

"Something like that. Except I have only one boss."

"Who's that?" Izzie asks.

"He doesn't live around here."

"What's your business?"

Mephisto smiles funny-like. His green eyes remind me of a cat's. I'm noticing all of a sudden how white and pointed all his teeth look. His lips are bright red. And the way his breath smells—more like he's been drinking kerosene than beer. "I have some accounts to collect," he says.

Izzie chuckles. "I'm retiring after today and, just for laughs, I'd like to see how you work, Mephisto. Can me and my friend come along and watch? You're dressed pretty nice and this is a tough neighborhood. You might need some extra muscle."

"That might prove beneficial," he says. I ain't never heard such cultural talk from a black man before. He makes

85

me and Izzie laugh right out loud. We follow him from the bar.

Two blocks south we see two men attempt to rob the First Tennessee Bank. The one with the money is running away, but the one with a gun is shooting at the security guard and he's firing back. "Stay out of this," Mephisto tells us.

The guard gets nicked on the arm, but his aim is better and he catches the felon in the chest. "Bastard," the guard says, "I hope you die and go to Hell!"

"Done!" Mephisto shouts. For an instant the robber's body flickers like a television screen when an airplane flies over the antenna. I have to rub my eyes. Then everything looks normal—except the robber is stone cold dead and Mephisto ain't around anymore. Then, while the security guard is checking the robber's body for a pulse, Mephisto pops up beside Izzie and me and drags us back about thirty yards.

"I'll be damned!" Izzie exclaims. "You *are* a magician."

"No," he says, "merely an obedient servant."

"For who?" Izzie asks.

"Why, the Devil, of course!"

"That can't be," Izzie says. "You're puttin' me on."

"Why do you think I had to leave and come back?" he asks. "It was to take that soul to Hell where the guard said he should go." To prove it, he lifts up his hat and shows us two tiny horns, one on each side of his head, just above his eyebrows.

"Damn!" Izzie declares. "I think I need another drink." So we head back to the bar.

About that time we come up on old Mr. Hollister, who's blind. His seeing eye dog Jake is a German shepherd about twelve years old with cataracts. Jake is almost as blind as Hollister, but Hollister won't get rid of him 'cause he's too attached to the pooch. Anyhow, Jake doesn't let Hollister know about a low-hanging Christmas sign and he walks right in to it and bangs his head pretty hard.

Yes, sir. I am leadin' up to something and I'm almost finished.

Hollister curses Jake a blue streak. Damns the poor old dog to hell and sounds like he's even been through it before personally.

Izzie laughs so hard it's a wonder he don't pee in his pants. "If you are a demon, why don't you claim that dog like you did the bank robber?" he asks.

With a smiling half-sneer, Mephisto answers, "Because he didn't mean it. See—" He points back at Hollister, who's kneeling down and pattin' the dog, soothing its hurt feelings after the cussin' its received. Now he's tellin' Jake he's forgiven and that he still loves him. Jake's waggin' his tail and lickin' Hollister's hand.

"That's what I mean," Mephisto says. "That is *'due process'* for us."

"So a curse means nothing unless it comes from the heart?" Izzie asks.

"Exactly."

As we head past the convenience store at Madison and Cleveland, who should come out but Mrs. Johnston with her meager little bag of groceries. Probably her Christmas Eve fixings to eat alone. Well, she sees Izzie and levels her gaze at him. She points a bony finger and says, "You're the no-good sumbitch who tricked me and served those papers. You're gonna get me thrown out of my home."

"Yes ma'am," Izzie says with pride. "All in a day's work."

"God damn you!" she says and starts walkin' off.

Izzie catches on quick. All the blood drains out of his face, even from his rum-blossom nose. "You don't mean that do you? I'm sorry, really. Forgive me. Please. Take it back."

"You go to Hell," she yells. "I do mean it and I'll never take it back."

Mephisto grabs Izzie's arm. "Come on, son," he says with an evil laugh, "we're going places."

Next thing I know, there's an explosion and I'm blown off my feet. Must have knocked me unconscious. I wake up and I'm lying there alone. Nobody knows how I got there. Nobody's seen Izzie since we left the bar. Nobody remembers the black dude.

Captain Mitchell, would you please make them turn me loose from this padded cell?

RETURN OF THE KING
(A FANTASY)

From her penthouse balcony Delilah watched the fog roll in from the river and enshroud downtown Memphis. The breeze offered no relief from the oppressive August heat.

She took a puff from her cigarette, sucked down what remained of her iced Scotch highball, and fought back the tears.

Occasionally she would hold the cold glass up against the ugly bruise on her temple, where one of the fans had pelted her with a dirt clod.

For this was another anniversary of HIS death, when all THE FANS came to mourn HIM. But, hadn't she, as HIS former stepmother, been a part of HIS LIFE, too?

This was *after* HIS father had divorced her and paid a king's ransom to make her go away forever, only she wouldn't. She dared not let the press know how she had stupidly squandered her settlement on slower horses, younger men, and older liquor.

With all the dirt she had spread about HIM—to Hell with whether or not it was true as long as it sold—she'd at least been able to convince three publishers as to her marketability.

Those first two books had done well. She had not taken royalties. This time she'd been smarter. Right when it seemed nobody had anything new to say about HIM, she'd made up some choice material. Naturally, it flattered her and made those she didn't like look bad. Very bad.

Her street smarts had told her to say bad things that weren't true only about those who were *dead*. Otherwise she might get sued.

She'd had no problem finding targets, from her late ex-husband (HIS father, whom she had met as a widower), to her predecessor (HIS real mother), to HIM (HIMSELF). All she had to do was open her mouth and the tabloids would go ga-ga, plus pay her big bucks.

Her concoctions had been more succulent than Cajun crawfish gumbo. First she insinuated that HE had been homosexual, or at least bisexual. That was probably what had earned her the dirt clod in the face today. Next she had exaggerated all out of proportion HIS involvement with drugs. Then she claimed that HIS death had been a suicide.

When none of the tabloids seemed willing to pay for any more of her wild revelations, she dropped the bombshell—her assertion that HE'D had an incestuous affair with HIS MOTHER! That sent the gossip mongers flocking with checkbook in hand.

Even tabloid readers have a threshold of tolerance. Delilah's incest line transgressed it.

All the fat ladies in stretchpants, waiting along with their balding husbands and whining grandchildren at the gates to HIS MANSION, must have read her stories. When she tried to pose for a publicity shot—after having been refused access to THE GROUNDS—they boo-ed and hissed at her.

Shouts arose from the crowd, "Judas! Traitor! Go away, you old witch!"

"But I loved HIM," she had cried. That was when the dirtball hit her.

Alone on the balcony of her hotel room, she wept. "Oh, why doesn't anyone think I loved YOU? IF only I could tell YOU face to face!"

The fog roiled up thick, so heavy she could barely see. She heard a rushing, soaring sound across the balcony, then footsteps—a man's.

The fog dissipated. Standing three feet away, she saw a familiar figure. When his lips curled into that trademark sneer of a smile, she knew it could only be HIM. Wearing a black jumpsuit and matching cape, with boots—traditional stage attire—HE looked so slim and trim, like HE'D stepped off the new commemorative stamp.

HIS familiar, husky voice warbled, "Are you lonesome tonight?"

She felt a rush of elation and fear. HE wasn't dead. HIS death had been a hoax! She could explain—make up a good lie—she'd been mistaken and was sorry. HE'D forgive her. Hadn't HE always before?

It shouldn't be hard. Hadn't HE always been a fool for a pretty face and a well-turned thigh? After her most recent facelift and total body lipo-suction, didn't she again possess the features of a girl in her mid-thirties? Well, almost!

All she had to do was *charm* HIM.

She shook her dyed blonde locks seductively and lowered the zipper on her white silk jumpsuit to expose her silicone-enhanced cleavage. She flicked the burning cigarette over the balcony and slunk enticingly toward HIM.

"I always *knew* you'd come back. Remember how much I *loved* you?"

The sneer on HIS lips became more pronounced as HE spoke, in a tone of contempt, the way HE had talked to the bad guys in HIS B-movies. "So you knew, huh?... How?"

She pressed close, enough to smell HIS natural musk scent mingled with the Aramis cologne HE always wore.

"You promised to take care of us—said we'd never want for anything. Then you died—so suddenly. Your will put everything in trust for your baby and cut us out. I had to make do *somehow*."

She moved to kiss and embrace HIM, but HE caught her arms and held her back. HIS blue eyes were smoldering. Was it with desire or anger?

"Is that why you sold those lies to the rag-sheets?" Menace resonated in HIS voice.

She felt threatened, yet—hadn't she always been able to handle HIM before? Like all men, HE was a sucker.

Batting her eyelids, she replied, "Why, darling, I don't know what you mean!"

HE reached inside HIS cape and withdrew a periodical with her picture on the front. "This."

The headlines proclaimed "**INTIMATE FAMILY SECRETS REVEALED.**"

She tried to recover her charm. "Dear, nobody takes that stuff seriously."

HE came close, towering over her, breathing rapidly, excitedly. In HIS familiar Southern drawl HE said, "*I do.*"

"Now don't go gettin' all worked up. Trust me. I'll publish a retraction—say I had a reaction to some prescription drugs. Your doctor always did make a good scapegoat!"

She drew close. This time HE did not resist. She whispered, "Oh, it feels so good to hold you. This wasn't right when your daddy was alive, but it's *okay* now."

She could feel HIS breath against her naked throat. HE was becoming aroused.

HE panted, "Thank you very much!" ...And sank HIS razor-sharp fangs into her throat.

She tried to struggle, but pleasure quickly overtook the pain. Exquisite pleasure, greater than any she had ever known. Now she knew *how* HE had come back—and she didn't care.

It made such perfect sense. HE'D always loved the night and shunned the day.

She felt the inseam of her pantsuit flood with the wetness of a torrential orgasm. Although weak, almost to the point of death, and reeling from loss of blood, she hoped this ecstacy would go on forever.

HE broke free and said with an evil laugh, "That's enough. Doc told me to watch my *junk food intake.*"

HE released her. Her life force ebbing away, she fell to the balcony floor. HE shook HIS head in mock remorse. "You shouldn't have said bad things about my Momma!"

As death overtook her, the fog rolled back in and HE disappeared.

At that same moment the cheap newspaper HE'D left behind blew across the balcony, and settled on her face.

CREDITS

"The Burrower from the Bluff" and "Due Process" have both been accepted by *Eldritch Tales* (Lawrence, Kansas) and will be released sometime in the foreseeable future. The author only released first serial rights and anthology rights were expressly retained.

"Return of the King" was included in *The King Is Dead: Tales of Elvis Postmortem* (Paul M. Sammon, ed.; Delta Books: New York, 1994).

ABOUT THE AUTHOR

Beecher Smith lives in Memphis, Tennessee with his family, including a Boston Terrier. He was an honor student at Millsaps College, where he majored in English literature before graduating and going to the University of Tennessee to earn his law degree. He distinguished himself in the practice of law as Elvis Presley's personal attorney, probated the late entertainer's will, and chartered Elvis Presley Enterprises. He rezoned Graceland to become a world-class museum and continues to be of counsel to the Presley family. After a near-fatal hunting accident in 1986, he returned to writing poetry and fiction, for which he has received numerous awards. The Poetry Society of Tennessee elected him its Poet Laureate in 1995. That same year he was inducted as a fellow Laureate Man of Letters by the United Poets Laureate International and the World Congress of Poets. His identical twin, Vassar Smith, also is a published poet.